I AM NOT AFRAID:
SCARY SITUATIONS AND OUTRAGEOUS EXPERIENCES

Loretta Brush Normile and Bryan Reeves

AuthorHouse™
1663 Liberty Drive
Bloomington, IN 47403
www.authorhouse.com
Phone: 1 (800) 839-8640

Published by AuthorHouse 06/25/2019

ISBN: 978-1-7283-1627-7 (sc)
ISBN: 978-1-7283-1628-4 (e)

Library of Congress Control Number: 2019907999

Print information available on the last page.

authorHOUSE®

Forword

Most kids don't want to get hurt or ill; but sometimes they do. Their injuries or illness may cause pain and discomfort, but it makes for a great story once it's finished! Back in the day, we compiled stories from classmates, family and children of colleagues. This collection, written during those vulnerable ages of 10-12 years, reflects their experiences as they were soothed, healed, and cared for by nurses.

We'd like to thank then 5th grade teacher Steve Bagiatis, West Hempfield Elementary School, Irwin, PA for encouraging students to participate and share their tales with the rest of us. We genuinely appreciate a grant from Epsilon Zeta Chapter, Sigma Theta Tau which made this collection of stories and book possible.

Finally, this book is dedicated to Dr. Maryanne Noble who was a nursing professor at George Mason University, and a psych-mental health nurse. Her keen intellect, insight and kindness inspired so many around her.

Bryan s Bike Mishap

by Bryan Reeves

On a hot summer day, I decided to ride my friend's bike. As I jumped on the shiny blue racer I thought that my friend's bike had foot brakes. It actually had hand brakes. Oh, no! I was pedaling straight towards our neighbor's big oak tree. I swerved away and then the bike swung around five times! I was trying to avoid hitting the neighbor's blue van. Instead I was propelled on top of a ledge as I kept on pedaling. My neighbor's huge red gasoline can was perched on the ledge so my neighbor could fill his lawn mower. I crashed into the gasoline can and fell what seemed to be like a long way…four feet down. I landed SMACK, face first onto their driveway. It was amazing. There were no smashes at all on the bike. But I had a big black and blue bruise on my left hand. Worse yet, my teeth went straight through my lip.

My mother and stepfather immediately took me to the emergency room at the local hospital. As the emergency room doors swung open, several nurses dressed in green scrub suits quickly came to help me. One nice nurse touched my hand and asked me how I was doing. I looked up at her with big scared eyes and did not answer. I was in so much pain. Even more so, I was very frightened about my lip and my hand. Thoughts raced through my head. Is my hand broken? Will they have to operate on me to fix my lip, which now felt as big a tire?

A nurse came in and calmly told me she was a nurse practitioner and she was going to put a bandage on my bruised hand and four stitches in my lip. That was really scary! The nurse gently talked to me as she numbed my lip with Novocain. As she told me a funny story, she quickly put the stitches into my lip. I didn't feel a thing! I didn't even know that nurses could sew up lips. I started to relax and feel safe. I managed to make it through all that without the tiniest twinge of pain! As I left the emergency room with my parents, I was amazed how certain kinds of nurses can sew up lips and be kind at the same time, and sometimes even funny.

Bee ing Kicked

by Remy Stone

My brother's graduation party was going to be the greatest! I was waiting weeks for the day to arrive. The beginning of summer, the end of the school year, and a party all at the same time, wow! I was especially excited since I knew there was going to be lots of cake. The party was a picnic in one of my favorite parks, a huge place with slides and swings. I was really looking forward to seeing so many friends and relatives and playing in the park with my sister and cousins.

On a sunny summer day with lots of people at the party, I remember wandering off with my cousin Leah and friend Jasmine to get a closer look at some of the pretty flowers and weeds, and curious bugs near the picnic pavilion While I was running through the park, I saw what looked like an old rotting baseball. It was stuck in a fence and I kicked it with my foot. Only then did I realize that what I thought was a rotting baseball was really a bee hive. Out they came...tons of bees! They were swarming all around me because I disturbed their hive. I hate bees! I have been really scared of them since I was very small. I ran for my life in the direction of the pavilion, screaming the whole time. I definitely tried to outrun these nasty bees, but one or more of the big ones stung me just above my right eyelid. I fell down onto the ground and a huge crowd of family, friends and people I never met before made a circle around me. Someone lifted me up and carried me over to a chair. By now my screaming was replaced by streams of big tears. My eye was burning, and I wasn't even sure why. My Aunt Margie instructed someone to bring my parents over immediately while Aunt Loretta calmly asked me to tell her what happened while inspected by my burning, painful eyebrow. I had been stung, at least once by the monster bees. Aunt Loretta ordered someone to get ice and clean napkins. She checked my eye and above my eyebrow where the swelling was starting. She asked me to be brave and calm and told me I didn't need to be afraid because she was a nurse and had seen many bee stings and knew just what to do. Aunt Loretta was gentle and thorough. She checked me all over to be sure there were no other bee stings. She put the ice over my eye and that helped ease the pain. When my parents came over, Aunt Loretta asked them if I had an allergy to bee stings and they said no. I was so happy! No trip to the hospital would be necessary! By this time, I was feeling much better from all the care and attention I was getting. My brother Mike came over and made a joke about the swelling. He said, "You look like you grew a third eye." He was really funny and made me laugh.

My Icy Fall

by Austin Khov

One winter day, after the snow turned to ice in 2007, I was out to take my dog Max, out for his *business* right before I went to school. I got out his leash and took him out to the back yard. While we were out it was really slippery, So when Max spotted the open door to the house, he pulled me right behind him. I fell down **hard**! As he pulled, I fell forward with my right leg twisted inward, and I slammed down with a *CRACK*! I was in so much pain I couldn't get up. I was on the ice laying there panicking, "Oh my gosh! What am I going to do?" But just as I was panicking I found my cell phone in my backpack and called my mom to come out and get me.

My mom was panicking! She was very scared, she called my dad and he raced back home, he was on his way to work. He got home within minutes and he raced to get me to the hospital. As I strolled in a wheelchair, the nurse came to see how I was doing. She was really kind and asked me how I was doing. It seemed like only a couple a minutes before the doctor got to see me. During the whole process of checking how bad my leg was, the doctor and the nurses were very caring and kind. They kept on asking me how I was feeling and told me they would help me if I was in discomfort. After a few x-rays, they told me my foot was fractured and I would have to have a cast on for a couple of months. The thing that really helped me get through the whole scary thing was the cool nurses!

My Scary Situation

by Megan Noble

The summer before sixth grade when I was 10 or 11, I was running as fast as my legs would move me. I was sliding down a pole on the playground...and then I felt it! It was like a big sharp pain. Every time I moved my head, my neck was in very bad pain. When I tried to turn to look, I inevitably started crying. That day, the camp staff came over to me and asked if I was okay. I couldn't shake my head "no" because my neck hurt so much so I let out a quiet "no." The camp staff took me to the campsite and called my mom.

All that was going through my mind was maybe I had broken a bone or twisted a joint in my neck or shoulder. I couldn't calm down because I was so frightened! I had no idea why my neck started hurting and how it had happened. My mom arrived and we drove to my doctor's office. My doctor wasn't in that day so a female nurse checked out my injury.

Her nice manner made me calm down and stopped my tears. She was very patient and asked me questions about how I hurt myself. Finally, she came up with a diagnosis and said, "You have pinched a nerve in you shoulder." I felt better knowing I hadn't broken a bone, but I didn't understand how a nerve in my shoulder could affect my neck. She took her time and explained it to me and it suddenly made sense to me. She told my mom to buy Motrin and to put ice on my shoulder. Even though in the beginning I was really scared, this nice nurse had calmed me down, told me it was only a minor injury, and that I would be okay. She made me feel better when I was unsure and scared.

When I Got Hurt

by Christen Frankhauser

When I was little, I got in a lot of trouble with my sister, Hannah. She's older than I am and way more adventurous. My sister and I were bored, and we had nothing to do. Hannah had a bright idea (which now I know was a very dumb idea). We named it "***the rock toss***". I know, it sounds ridiculous already. We started off by getting four buckets. Hannah had two buckets, both full of clay or small rocks. I, at the other end, had two buckets with nothing in them. Hannah, who has the rocks, throws them into the bucket I'm holding. When my one bucket was full, I wanted to switch it with the other bucket. When I was not looking, my sister said, "Watch out!" So, I got up and said "What?" That's when it started. All I saw was the rock coming at me, and I just stood there not knowing what to do. All of a sudden, the solid, soaring rock hit me in the head. Believe it or not, I did not cry! When my mom saw my sister throwing rocks, she ran down the porch steps and yelled at Hannah to stop it. My mom then went to see what I was doing. When she saw that there was blood on the sidewalk, she checked my body to see where it was coming from. Then she found out that it was from my head. When she said that I was bleeding, I started crying because I was scared.

Meanwhile, my dad was home and my mom quickly ran through the door and told my dad that I was bleeding really bad from my head. So my dad replied, "I think we should take her to the hospital, just in case." I think my whole family took me to the hospital. We rushed into the car and zoomed as fast as we could to the hospital. As the emergency room doors opened, we quickly went to the room where they put staples in. After my staples were in, we went back home.

A couple of weeks later, I could take them out. Since I was only four, I could not remember everything in the hospital. To take the staples out, I did not go to the hospital. My Aunt Cathy is a nurse so I went to her house down the street, so we wouldn't have to go the whole way to the hospital. When we got to my aunt's house, I did not know she was taking the staples out. When I did find out, I ran out the door and ran around the house. When I saw my sister, I ran the opposite way. But, as I kept going, my cousin, Claire, was on the other side. I realized that I was blocked in, so I ran straight. I thought I was safe. When I looked back, no one was there. When I looked forward again, I saw my other cousin, Leah, standing there in front of me. When I looked to my right, I saw my sister Hannah, and when I turned around, there was Claire! I knew then that I had to get the staples pulled out. After they all took me inside the house, they sat me down on a chair. Then, my mom held me on the chair so I wouldn't move while Aunt Cathy took the staples out. I was crying because I knew it was going to hurt. Then a second later, it was all done. I was so incredibly scared for nothing. The experience wasn't anywhere near as bad as I thought it would be, but I'm not going to play any more risky games with my sister again!

The Day I Went to the Hospital

by Kyle Devers

It was my tenth birthday, and we had a bunch of snow on the ground. Naturally, I went sledding down my back yard with all of its many hills. I got a running start and WHOOSH! As I zoomed down the hill, my sled curved and I went flying in mid-air. It was just my luck that I landed in a pine tree. I was covered in needles and looked like a porcupine! After I got out of the prickly, pointy pine trees my mom took me to the hospital and they rushed me to the emergency room. They took the pointy pine needles out of me and then they gave me two stitches in a really bad cut. That day really hurt but I made it through it. The kind nurse made sure I was feeling better and she said that I would get the stitches out in about 2 weeks. It wasn't exactly a happy birthday, but it was quite the adventure!

How My Bike Adventure Turned Into a Trip to the Hospital

by Matt Zitkovich

One day I was riding my brand new motorbike near the railroad tracks with my cousin. He was following me with his new YZ250 and my uncle was on a dirt bike in front of me. I crossed a road, hit a jump, and lost my balance. Then it happened...I ran my street tires into a pothole on the road. I lost control and my bike slid out from under me. It felt like I was falling off a building rather than a dirt bike! I fell on a pile of sharp rocks and boy did I get cut up! I had a major open cut on my arm. I rode the YZ250 racing bike back to the car. I looked down at my stomach and saw that there was a huge brush burn there. My leg was torn up, and my finger was twisted and bent. I had my uncle rush me to the hospital. The nurse gave me shots in my arm that made the pain stop. I didn't even feel it. When I woke up, I was still hurting. The nurse came in and I said, "Thanks." I held her hand with a hard grip. I felt safe. She told me I was in good hands. She said, "You will be alright now," and I trusted her enough to know she was right.

The Tree Mishap

by Megan Gaza

One day I was playing outside in my huge backyard. My sister came out and wanted to wash her playhouse. I didn't want to help so I decided to climb a tree instead. This was no little tree! It was taller than my house. So, I started climbing until I was about half of the way up the tree. Then, I heard a snap! That is when my hand slipped off the branch. I fell what seemed like hundreds of feet. I broke my upper arm and it really hurt badly. Even today my arm isn't perfectly straight. I found myself lying on the ground in so much pain. Then my grandma came over and helped me up. She and my mom had to rush me to the hospital. At the hospital, a nurse approached me and asked if everything was okay. She was very nice. I remember her name.... Nurse Cathy. But the hospital was so very busy, so I had to wait in the waiting room before I could get my arm treated. I sat there and worried that I might have to get my arm amputated (cut off). The nurse gave me an ice pack to put on my arm while I waited. Finally, it was my turn to go into an exam room. Nurse Cathy kindly escorted me there and sat on the bed talking to me softly while we waited for the doctor. I must have looked really frightened. That was the nicest nurse I ever met.

My Accident

by Kaninta "Addy" Esmeralda

One hot summer's day, I was walking with my aunt to buy ice cream for the both of us. When I was walking, I tripped over a rock and smack, I fell on my back! A motorcycle was zooming down the street… and it was too late to get up! My aunt tried to help get me up, but the motorcycle was only about five inches away from my knee! The tires of the motorcycle skid on my knee and my leg was gushing blood all over the road!! That freaked me out. The driver asked my aunt where I lived, and when he got to my house, he told my mom what happened. My aunt stayed with me to keep me comforted. My mom rushed me in to our car to get me to the emergency room. It was scary!

As my mom and I rushed through the emergency room, my white shorts turned all red from the bleeding! The nurse, wearing light blue scrubs, told me I would need stitches. I was only five years old. Scary thoughts raced through my head. The nurse gave me a lollipop to keep my mind off getting stitches. She told me to think about happy thoughts, or thoughts about eating ice cream. By the time she was done, I fainted! I guess I was shocked that it didn't hurt. By the time I woke up, I was in my car. My mom told me the nurse gave me an extra lollipop for being brave! Yum!!!

Shots!

by Jessica Mosher

I got three shots. It hurt but the nurse was so kind. I was only supposed to get one shot but my mom thought it was good to get two more. The nurse said to calm down and just look or talk to your mom. Before she gave me the shots she wiped the place where she was going to give me the shots. It was cold. So, she gave me the shots and it did not hurt because I was distracted. She said, "Good job," and patted me on my back.

When I Went to See a Nurse.

by Anthony Ciorra

One time I was catching baseball with my friends. When one threw it to me, it hit my pinky when I caught it. My pinky started to swell up. Another friend threw it and it hit my pinky again. After this time, my pinky started to hurt. Then after my friends left I went inside and noticed that my one pinky was fatter than the other and it was sore too.

When I went in I told my mom what happened since she was a nurse. She said that I probably jammed my finger. So, my mom made a splint for my finger so it could not bend that way. It could heal. Eventually, it healed all thanks to my mom, the nurse!

A Bad Day

by Amanda Jepsen

I was feeling horrible all day, because my stomach was churning all around. I was as white as a ghost and my eyes were closing with every blink. When I went to lunch, I was standing in line very patiently until all of a sudden, I felt a tickle in my throat. Oh, no! You can guess what happened after that and I let loose on my friend Mary. I ran out of the room all scared and frightened. A lunch lady found me and took me to the school nurse.

She was very, very nice. First, she said, "Good thing you did not get your pretty outfit all dirty, but you did get it on your friend." The nurse asked if I wanted to lay down, I said yes, and she helped me onto the bed because it was kind of high. She gave me a glass of water and took my temperature… it was 100 degrees. She called my mom and talked to me about school with questions like "Who is your teacher? Do you like sports?" That was the best nurse I ever met.

Printed in the United States
By Bookmasters